Once Upon a Time in
LITHUANIA

NAOMI ALEXANDER

Once Upon a Time in
LITHUANIA

DAVID
PAUL

First Published in Great Britain in 2006 by

DAVID PAUL
25 Methuen Park
London
N10 2JR

www.davidpaulbooks.com

Copyright © Naomi Alexander. All artworks are the copyright of the artist, Naomi Alexander.

All rights reserved. No part of this publication may be reproduced, stored in a retrieval system or transmitted by any other means, electronic, mechanical, photocopying, recording or otherwise, without the prior permission in writing of the publishers, nor be otherwise circulated in any form of binding or cover other than that in which it is published and without a similar condition including this condition being imposed on the subsequent purchaser.

Designed and produced by

PAPADAKIS PUBLISHER
an imprint of New Architecture Group Ltd
16 Grosvenor Place, London SW1X 7HH

www.papadakis.net

Design Director: Alexandra Papadakis
Designer: Shirlynn Chui

Copyright © 2006 Papadakis Publisher. All rights reserved.

A CIP catalogue of this book is available from the British Library.

ISBN 0 954848 21 7

The publication of this book would not have been possible without the generous support of the Association of Baltic Jews in Great Britain, the descendants of the Feiges family and other donors.

Distribution by Central Books, 99 Wallis Road, London E9 5LN

Printed in Singapore

Contents

Acknowledgements	7
Foreword Lord Janner of Braunstone, QC	8
The art of painting Jewish Lithuania Naomi Alexander	9
Naomi Alexander in Lithuania John Russell Taylor	10
The Litvaks: The Jews of Lithuania Professor Aubrey Newman	12
Lithuania: A historical timeline	14
List of towns	16
Map of Lithuania	18
Sketches and paintings	19
Catalogue of Works	156
References and Credits	160

In loving memory of my mother and father,
Hazel and John Alexander.

Acknowledgements

I am especially grateful to Gintaras Karosas, president of Lithuania's Europas Parkas Open Air Museum for the Centre of Europe who offered me an artist's residency in 2001 and supported my wish to paint Jewish culture; and to his wife, Lina, who looked after me so well. Thank you also to the Vilna Gaon Museum's chief curator Rosa Bielioskiene, whose patience, interest and guidance were invaluable, and others who guided me, such as Regina Kopilevich, whose home I stayed in and who took me around Kaunas, and Dovydas Leibzonas, who guided me in Kedainiai. Thank you also to Lord Janner and the Holocaust Educational Trust for showing me places that I would never otherwise have discovered; to Alvgis Mulvinskas at the Town Hall, Kretinga for supplying me with old photographs; Flo Kaufmann JP, vice president of the Board of Deputies of British Jews, for her wise advice and to Lionel Kopelowitz, Saul Issrof and Julia Weiner for their support and interest, and who gave advice when I needed it. Thank you also to my family for putting up with my constant obsessive eccentricites and allowing me to flourish in my own chaotic way, especially my sisters Katrina and Fabia, my brother Anton and his wife Stella, who eased my loneliness in the forests of Lithuania; to my daughter Georgia for being my endless support and strength, and my grandchildren Alexandra and Boris, for their love, help and encouragement. I would also like to express my thanks to my publisher David Paul, whose sympathetic interest was so helpful in turning what might have been just a catalogue into something that has become much more interesting. Thank you also to Alexandra Papadakis and her team at Papadakis Publisher for the bold and imaginative design, and to the book's contibutors, Professor Aubrey Newman and John Russell Taylor, for their supportive words and giving of their time. Not least I am immensely grateful to the Association of Baltic Jews in Great Britain, the descendants of the Feiges family and other donors for their generous financial contributions. And finally my thanks to all the people who were kind enough and brave enough to allow me into their homes to draw.

Naomi Alexander, 2006

Foreword

Lithuania is – sadly – literally as well as metaphorically my family graveyard. So I welcome Naomi Alexander's unique and remarkable book, with its moving paintings and sketches of that tragic land.

Through the Holocaust Educational Trust, I have been working for years to find, to access, to map and mark and signpost the Baltic mass graves. We have found over 200 in Lithuania and nearly 100 in Latvia. In the early 1940s the Nazis – too often with the help of local sympathisers – rounded up the Jews and herded them out into the forests or deserted parts of cities. They dug deep ditches, shot and buried their victims – and then returned and took over their homes and property. Without our work we "Litvaks" would have lost the memories for ever. And without the work of Naomi Alexander, there would be little memory for the more human and happier history of that assorted heritage. The artist throws light onto the lives of our ancestors, before their deaths, and gives us pictorial glimpses of our past.

I have made many visits to Lithuania, both political and for our Mass Graves Project, and have seen most of the sites – and the sights – so well captured by Naomi Alexander in this book. And I am happy to recommend it to all who wish to catch a glimpse of a Jewish world so sadly destroyed.

Greville Janner
(Lord Janner of Braunstone, QC)

The art of painting Jewish Lithuania

Naomi Alexander

When I had the opportunity of an artist's residency at the Europas Parkas Museum in Vilnius, I knew immediately I wanted to draw Jewish culture. My grandmother's family had come from Darbenai (Dorbian) near the north-west border and the family tree stretches back to the mid-18th century. My mother was a sculptor and one of her most powerful creations shows Jews rushing away on horses and carts escaping from Lithuania before the First World War. We always talked of visiting and finding out more about where we came from.

I felt intensely the presence of the Jews that once lived there, the homes they lived in, the things they must have done and the places they visited, and there is a sense that I am commemorating their lives here.

I want people to see what the shtetls and towns are like, but my drawings are not exact replications, they are not photographs. Photographs can give you a lot of information but one is left with a much colder feeling. By taking away the straight lines of buildings, for instance, by curling the roofs, a different kind of reality emerges that I hope is warmer and more powerful. Whereas, in a darker drawing, where Nazi atrocities occurred – at the Ninth Fort, a difficult subject to draw – I have left some parts of the walls blank, simply to make the picture less busy.

I prefer to draw quickly. In one sketch there is a broken-down chapel, a bundle of wood. It would have taken several hours to sketch accurately but after four or five minutes' drawing it is etched in my memory. It becomes my diary. It is how I remember. In a pencil drawing I remember the detail, a crack in the corner of a building, a mood. Even more so if I paint, for that takes longer. But if I take too long over a painting it becomes too architectural with too much precision, and the emotion is lost.

I like naivety, I would like to be a child in the way I paint. I would like not to see perspective and obliterate it.

I am interested in the illusion that can be created just by drawing the shape of a person. I enjoy drawing women, simply because the clothes they wear tend to be softer and flowing and I can keep a line going and I can make the lines link up, which happens in all my drawings.

Several of my models here are non-Jewish Lithuanian peasant women in their homes, but as I draw them I cannot help but imagine the Jewish mothers that would have once lived there. In one of my triptychs a Lithuanian woman in a pink pinafore is my model. But I have my daughter's hands blessing the Friday night candles. That seemed appropriate and I continually alter reality if it feels right. So my granddaughter appears in the backdrop to a kitchen like some shtetl child. And similarly with landscapes, I will change things as I feel appropriate and for design and balance.

I am attracted to domestic objects. I am obsessed by old ovens and kitchens. Perhaps this is because I went to art school in the '60s when the kitchen-sink painters like John Bratby were in vogue. But I have probably been even more influenced by Vuillard and Bonnard, post-impressionist painters who can capture a moment with simple brushstrokes. And I can identify with the humour and honesty in the epigraph Bonnard used at one exhibition to describe his way of painting: "Lots of little lies for the sake of one big truth".

Naomi Alexander in Lithuania

John Russell Taylor

Most people who talk about something or someone being "beyond the pale" do not give a second thought to what the phrase literally means. The two most famous pales historically were the Pale that separated the English from the Irish in Ireland, which was intended as a hedge or boundary, as it kept the Irish out of the English-settled territories; and the Pale designed by Catherine the Great to keep the Jews inside the territories where they had settled before the partition of Poland. The vast majority of Jews then remained in what are now Latvia, Lithuania, the Ukraine and Eastern Poland, where they had already lived for centuries. This was the country, in other words, of Fiddler on the Roof and Yentl. From these films in particular we have a strong visual image of what life was like then for the inhabitants of these outsider regions.

But we probably do not imagine for a moment that it could possibly be anything like that now, in the 21st century. But what is it like? Naomi Alexander, whose family came to Britain from Lithuania (her husband's family came around the same time from Latvia), wanted to know, and set out for the recently liberated Baltic states in search of her roots. These drawings are the product of her quest.

The first thing to be said about them is that they capture a world which looks amazingly as it must have a century ago. The second is that there is one radical difference: there are no Jews. Alexander finds the village her grandparents came from. She even finds the house in which they lived. There are still synagogues, carefully preserved and sometimes lovingly restored. But the synagogues are more museum than anything else, and the villages, the houses, are as they were primarily because the Gentiles who have taken them over are just as poor as their Jewish predecessors, and cannot afford to update and import modern conveniences.

Hence the feeling one receives that these drawings open a window on to the past. They do, perhaps, embody a vestigial nostalgia, but Alexander firmly disapproves of the kind of self-conscious preservationism that is now turning many places in Eastern Europe into exotic equivalents of Disneyland. What interests her, in the drawings at least, is precise recording of what she has seen and the way she has seen it. Throughout her career, Alexander has eschewed excessive emotion, maintaining a classical distance, which allows her to deconstruct and reconstruct her images, distilling the emotion inherent in the subject, only to re-create it through strictly artistic means.

But, you may say, surely it must be impossible for a Jewish artist to visit an area so heavily charged with emotion, virtually at the gates of some of the more notorious Nazi death camps, without succumbing to the whole weight of history, personal as well as general. If you emphasise the "Jewish" that may well be so. But what if you emphasize the "artist"? And whatever else she may be, Alexander is first and foremost an artist. She is the last to wish to be corralled into some specialised area labelled "woman artist", "Jewish artist", "British artist" or whatever. And she performs the duty of an artist: to embody a personal vision in a work of art which automatically detaches itself from its maker and requires to be judged in its own terms.

So it is with these drawings. True, they are – as they give the impression of being – spontaneous. But that does not mean that the process of artistic distillation has not taken place. One must remember Whistler's defence against Ruskin's charge that he had just thrown a pot of paint at the canvas: that any painting he might do at that stage in his career took the possibly short time he stood, brush in hand, in front of the canvas, plus the forty years' experience it had taken him for doing it to become second nature.

Alexander's art, for all its frequent spontaneity, always places proper weight on the fundamental brain work. Some of the paintings inspired by her time in the Baltics, such as those suggested by old photographs of her husband's family which document traditional patterns of Jewish life, have the gravity of slow and conscious discipline. But there are others, such as a series depicting the high, arched room where she lived and worked in Lithuania, that edge towards abstraction in their directness, speed and simplicity. And when we come to the sketchbook drawings, the on-the-spot quality is instantly self-evident, along with the advantages of an artistic discipline which guides the hand even as the mind is most moved by what the eye sees.

It is revealing to compare the Baltic drawings with an earlier series which arose from circumstances which could hardly have been more different. A little while ago Alexander was invited by the Duke of Devonshire to paint at Chatsworth, and in preparation she spent some time sketching there. Even then, be it noted, she was not pinning down on paper the grandeurs that everyone associates with one of the great aristocratic seats of Britain, but poking around the detritus of generations left gathering dust in the attics. The Chatsworth sketches are magical in their evocation of these neglected, private spaces: all the atmospheric essentials are there, captured in a moment.

The attics were uninhabited, virtually deserted, relying for their emotional effect on the bittersweet charms of broken furniture and abandoned toys. But around the same time, Alexander went outdoors to make a series of watercolours, a form of painting which retains the immediacy of drawing. These thumbnail sketches of people bathing on sparsely populated beaches have all the lightness and humour and humanity of the moment as it flies.

The Lithuanian drawings combine the distinct qualities of the Chatsworth drawings and the seaside watercolours. Given the circumstances of their making and the emotional impetus behind them, one might expect the drawings exploratory of Alexander's Jewish roots beyond the Pale to be grim, looking back, if not in anger, then at least in intense sadness. But this proves rarely if ever to be so. What interests Alexander above all are the evidences of life – life back then, but also life right this moment.

She delights in the primitive houses of her ancestors and their kind, the still unchanged peasant kitchens and scrubby gardens supporting a few chickens pecking among the rows of vegetables. Not because they are quaint, but because they are the most vivid evidence of things as they were, life as it used to be lived, and, life as it is still lived. The Jewish inhabitants may have long gone, but their Gentile, Catholic successors still carry on an almost identical lifestyle, scraping a living from the land and hoping that better days are just round the corner. Any sadness at their very presence is balanced by appreciation of and respect for the unconquerable vitality of the human spirit.

There is sentiment here, to be sure, but there is also humour and quirky observation. Alexander's relish of these old peasant women's foibles reminds us of her attitude to the bathers on the beach, all briskly captured in their human simplicity and complexity. At the same time, the dusty remnants of things long gone take us back to the Chatsworth attics: buildings and objects too have their hidden life, and carry with them evidences of their chequered history. It sometimes seems that the more spontaneous and, in a way, uncensored the artist's notation of what is seen, the more intense becomes that mysterious telepathy between artist and observer which enables the observer to see not only what the artist has seen, but also what she has seen in it.

Clearly Alexander's reasons for going to Lithuania were an intricate fusion of the conscious and the unconscious. Nostalgia is perhaps hardly the word, given all that happened to the relatives who remained until the Holocaust, but desire to make contact with the scenes and lives of her ancestors was obviously the strongest and most immediate purpose. And even though there was much to regret in the impoverished lives of the Jews in the Russian Pale at the start of the 20th century, there was also much to celebrate in their strong sense of community, of families unscattered, of religion joyously shared. The synagogues may now be empty, but their message lives on.

At the same time, there must have been some attraction to the intense exoticism of the country and the people for Alexander's generation to stir her interest and inspire her art. Not quite a tourist, not really a native returned, she must have reacted with a strange tangle of emotions – of delight and horror, of strangeness and familiarity. And all these sentiments are powerfully present in the drawings. They tell us much about the place and the people. They tell us much about the artist and how her heart and mind work. And even more, they tell us all that is tellable about the ways of art.

John Russell Taylor is the art critic of *The Times*.

The Litvacks: The Jews of Lithuania

Aubrey Newman

All over the world Jews characterise themselves less in terms of the land in which they live, more in terms of the land from which their parents, grandparents, or even those further back emigrated. Even where they no longer form associations linked with the areas of former settlement they still boast of their antecedents. And of no group is this more true than of the Litvacks, the Jews of Lithuania. To be able to claim to have come from the Kovno or Suwalki Guberniya (province) was to be almost an aristocrat. This was the land of the yeshivas, where learning was highly prized and seminaries were plentiful, where it is hard for a respected Litvack not to find a rabbi or a learned Rav somewhere in the family tree, as Naomi Alexander has found.

"Lithuanian Jewry" by long usage represents not merely the Jews living within the boundaries of the state of Lithuania as it existed during the 20th century but those of "Historic" Lithuania, the territories of the old grand duchy of Lithuania, at one stage extending from the Black Sea to the Baltic. Jews came into Lithuania by invitation of its rulers during the 14th century and included merchants and artisans, scholars and teachers, wealthy individuals and persons living in the deepest poverty. Initially they were accorded significant privileges and were certainly protected from the waves of anti-Jewish feeling which spread over much of the rest of Europe in that century. A charter was granted to the Jews in Lithuania in 1388 and 1389. They were given property rights, allowed to trade in liquor and engage in peddling, and allowed to work as artisans, and to dwell wherever they liked. They came under the protection of the ruler and were given special status in the law courts, and given the right to hear their own civil cases, except where one of the parties demanded a hearing before the grand duke's court. The Jews received the privileges of freedom of trade, the right to manufacture and sell alcohol, and the right to slaughter cattle in order to sell meat.

Over the succeeding centuries, even when there were to be edicts of expulsion, they were short-lived, for the Jews already played an essential role in the economy and the governance of Lithuania. As a consequence the various Jewish communities in Lithuania, like their co-religionists in Poland, were granted a considerable degree of autonomy. In Poland the "Council of the Four Lands" was set up, while in Lithuania the Council of Lithuania was established. By the beginning of the 17th century the Grand Duchy of Lithuania, now linked with the Kingdom of Poland, had expanded towards the Ukraine and Belorussia. The Jews played an important role in the economic development of these additional territories, becoming involved in agriculture and artisan trades, and dealing in livestock. They held brewing and distilling rights, and their communities spread over the whole region. Their role was largely that of being the bailiffs and agents of the land-owning nobility, and they were to pay a hard price for playing the role of middlemen. In 1648 and the two years following, a revolt broke out in the south of the Kingdom, largely amongst the Ukrainian Cossacks and led by Bogdan Chmielnicki. Tens of thousands of Jews were murdered and others were taken prisoner by the Cossacks and their allies. These disasters hit mainly the Jews in the south of the Grand Duchy but its effects were felt indirectly also by many communities in Lithuania proper, called on to assist the survivors from towns and villages which had been destroyed and whose inhabitants had been massacred.

However, the 18th century in general saw substantial developments amongst the Jewish communities in Lithuania, above all in their religious and cultural life. Scholars had begun moving to Lithuania from outside and the rabbi had become a respected and influential figure in the community. So eminent was Vilna and its seminaries that it was commonly known as "The Jerusalem of Lithuania".

By the end of the 18th century there were probably 120,000 Jews in Lithuania, widely dispersed amongst its various provinces and regions. A growing disintegration of the Polish-Lithuanian state and short-lived attempts at reform led to a dissolution of the Council of Lithuania and the loss of autonomy for the various Jewish communities. Nonetheless Poland fell victim to the greed of its neighbours. Its partition amongst them during the late 18th century brought the Jews of Lithuania under Russian control, and the fundamentally anti-Jewish attitudes of the Russian church and state resulted in a catastrophic deterioration of the conditions under which the Jews existed. The Jews were placed under an increasing number of restrictions affecting their occupations and places of residence. The Russian government imposed the hated and feared conscription, which involved military service for a minimum period of twenty five years, and which hit the community hard. The imposition of severe governmental restrictions on residence hit the country districts in particular. The result was a constant flow from the villages into the towns of Lithuania, large and small alike. The result was a growing, desperate poverty and unemployment.

Alexander II (1856 – 81), eased earlier restrictions, such as the conscription and the expulsions from frontier provinces or restrictions on residence in Kovno or Vilna, but the assassination of Alexander II in 1881 and the accession of the reactionary Alexander III brought a large-scale outburst of pogroms in the south, and although the governor of Lithuania prevented organised persecution in his province there were a number of anonymous arson attacks and violent incidents elsewhere. The imposition of the "Temporary" Laws in May 1882 increased the pressure on the Jews to move into the towns, while further restrictions on their possible occupations – such as denying them any share in the liquor trade – increased their poverty. Between the middle and the end of the 19th century the Jewish population almost tripled. The number of births remained high and mortality rates declined. In Vilna the Jewish population rose threefold. Kovno Guberniya was the most populous centre of life. The number of Jews in the province rose from 81,505 in 1847 to 115,911 in 1864, and to 212,666 in 1897. In the city of Kovno the numbers rose from 2,013 in 1847 to 25,448 in 1897. In many of the small towns Jews represented a majority of the whole population. This was despite an enormous emigration to Western Europe, the United States, and South Africa. Between 1881 and 1914 over 80,000 Jews left the Kovno province alone.

In April 1915 the Russian government ordered the expulsion of over 120,000 Jews from Lithuania on the grounds that they had been assisting the Germans in World War One, but by September the Russians had been forced out of Lithuania and it had come under German occupation. Further defeat in the war forced the collapse of the Russian state, and in 1918 Lithuania declared its independence. The condition of the Jews at first seemed to have improved and the new government gave official autonomy to the Jewish communities. But Poland seized Vilna and right-wing elements began to introduce anti-Semitic legislation. A coup d'état in 1926 marked the end of democracy in Lithuania, and the political and economic position of the 150,000 Jews there steadily worsened. The advent of the Nazis in Germany resulted in steady pressure on Lithuania. The signing in January 1939 of a German-Lithuanian non-aggression pact did not stop the Germans taking over the sole Lithuanian port of Klaipedia (Memel), and the Russo-German pact of August 1939 left Lithuania and the other Baltic states to Russian mercies, even though the Russians organised the restoration of Vilna to Lithuanian control. In 1940 the Russians took over direct control of Lithuania, and although some Jews welcomed the arrival of the Russians many more of the Jews (and the non-Jews) were regarded with suspicion by the Russians. Between 14th and 22nd June 1941 some 30,000 Lithuanians, many of them Jews, were deported to Siberia as "enemies of the state". Ironically, this was to save their lives, for it was on 22nd June 1941 that the Germans attacked. Within weeks tens of thousands of Lithuanian Jews had been slaughtered, many of them by Lithuanians. In August, for example, in Kovno alone some 4,000 Jews had been massacred even before the Germans arrived. Ghettos were established in Shavli, Vilna, and Kovno; in Kovno Dr Elhannan Elkes was elected as Head of the Ghetto, in which post he fought valiantly if unsuccessfully against the murder of 11,000 Jews in Fort Nine on the outskirts of Kovno, while in Vilna Jacob Gens saw the murder of thousands in Ponary. When in July 1944 Russian troops re-entered Lithuania they found that only some 10,000 Lithuanian Jews survived out of the 220,000 living there in June 1941. Over the next year these Jews were joined by many of the survivors of the concentration camps, while others remained in the West perpetuating the memory of those who had perished. In 1947 at a meeting of the Association of Lithuanian Jews there was a declaration:

> We, the few remnants of Lithuanian Jewry, are living testimony of the Lithuanians' cruelty to their Jewish neighbours. Each one of us can recount many facts concerning the unspeakable murders of innocent and helpless Jews perpetrated by the Lithuanian people during the occupation. … Every part of Lithuanian society … actively collaborated with the murderers in the destruction of Lithuanian Jewry.

An initial attempt at rebuilding Jewish life in Lithuania by opening schools and a Jewish museum in Kovno and Vilna ended by 1950, and there was a return of the active antisemitism of the pre-war years. However the death of Stalin presaged a partial amelioration of conditions and Jews began to move there from elsewhere in the Soviet Union. By 1989 there were over 12,000 Jews in Lithuania of whom almost half had been born elsewhere. But here again the rise of a new attitude in Russia, "Glasnost" changed opinions towards Jews. Revived Lithuanian nationalism brought attacks on those allegedly responsible for Soviet crimes against "loyal citizens", and this served as a cloak for further attacks on Jews who, it was claimed, had been responsible for the deportation of many Lithuanians. The results are shown by the statistics. In 1989 there were 12,314 Jews noted as living in Lithuania; in 1998 there were 4,500.

In recent years the Lithuanian government has been making attempts to revive memories of its Jewish population and to rehabilitate its reputation. Museums and cemeteries have been restored and there are attempts to come to a fresh understanding of the Jewish contribution to the history of the country. There are still problems, however, not the least being that of the ownership of properties which had been Jewish before 1941, now in non-Jewish hands but which the former owners wish to reclaim.

Survivors of Lithuanian Jewry say there is no Jewish future in Lithuania and that the Jewish community that lived and thrived in Lithuania for hundreds of years has been destroyed and will never rise again. Only those descended from those many Litvacks who were able to emigrate and create as it were Lithuanias in exile, be it in America, Israel, South Africa or Great Britain, can still retain some of the memory of those communities. Many of them go back on some sort of pilgrimage, look at the remains of Jewish habitation, but there is no return. The Jerusalem of Lithuania is desolate and her glories are no more.

Professor Newman is Honorary Associate Director of the Stanley Burton Centre for Holocaust Studies, University of Leicester and he is also Professor Emeritus at the university.

Lithuania: A historical timeline
Aubrey Newman

1323 Grand Duke Gediminas, Empire builder of Lithuania, makes Vilnius his capital and invites into his country Jews who come in part from south-east Europe, Germany and central Europe.

1386 Marriage of Gediminas' grandson, Yagiello (WladislawII) to Hedwig-Yadviga of Poland and union of Poland and Lithuania.

1388 Prince Vytautas of Lithuania grants an official charter to Jews of Troki and Brisk; synagogues and cemeteries are exempted from taxation and Jews given personal and religious security. The following year it was extended to Grodno. It laid the foundation for a system of Jewish autonomy and the basis of the structure for Jewish life between the 14th and 18th centuries.

1392 Vytautas invites Jews and Karaites to settle in Vilnius.

1401 Vytautas proclaims the autonomy of Lithuania.

1444 Poland and Lithuania again united under Casimir the Great.

1492 Casimir's successor, Alexander Yagiello, Grand Duke of Lithuania, expels the Jews from Lithuania and confiscates their property.

1503 Readmission of the Jews into Lithuania and appointment of Abraham Boemas as Senior and Judge of the Jews.

1528 Exclusion of Jews from Vilnius and Kaunas but many Jews moved into districts near the city owned by nobles and not under the control of the burghers of Vilnius and some Jews were appointed to important economic positions.

1551 Under Sigismund II recognition and enlargement of the powers of the Kahal, the Lithuanian Jewish Community Council.

1569 Union of Lublin, harmonising and merging the Polish and Lithuanian administrations. The Jews are now recognised as important in the economic system, becoming tax collectors and estate managers.

1573 First official synagogue in Vilnius.

1581 Official recognition of the 'Council of the Four Lands' – the Synod of the Provinces into which Jewish Poland was divided – Little Poland, Greater Poland, Belorussia, and Lithuania. This does not replace the individual *kehillot*, but becomes the official channel between the community and the government, thus ensuring autonomy.

1587 Election of Sigismund III as King of Poland and Grand Duke of Lithuania. During his reign the Jews become much more active as partners of the nobility, even sometimes becoming part owners of land. Many engage in money lending but others are active in agriculture and administration of estates as well as holding brewing and distilling rights. The nobility begin to create large numbers of small private townships *(shtetlakh)* wherein there were also many Jewish inhabitants, sometimes a majority.

1648 The Cossack uprising under Bogdan Chmielnicki was directed against the Poles and Jesuits, but the Jews also become targets, as the agents and bailiffs of the hated landlords. The murder of the Jews by the Cossacks was the most ferocious onslaught upon them until modern times. Thousands of Jews fled from the Ukraine to Lithuania, but then the Russians and Swedes invaded Lithuania.

1734 Great Fire of Vilna, the Jerusalem of Lithuania. Although many of the (wooden) houses and synagogues were destroyed they were soon rebuilt with assistance being given from Jewish communities all over Western Europe.

1764 Loss of Jewish autonomy by the Governmental dissolution of the Council of the Four Lands and the Council of Lithuania; however the individual community councils *(Kehillot)* were retained as a method of collecting taxation from the Jews.

1765 First census of Lithuanian Jews (Official figures 76,474; estimate 120,000).

1768 The Gaon (Rabbi Elijah ben Judah Solomon Zalman) settles in Vilna.

1772-1795 Partition and disappearance of an independent Poland/Lithuania; absorption into the Russian state.

1781 *Herem* (decree of religious excommunication) by the Gaon against the Hassidim and the rise in Lithuania of the *mitnaggedim* (opponents of Hassidism).

1812 Napoleonic invasion of Russia and short-term occupation of Vilnius.

1823 Establishment of "The Committee for Jewish Affairs" by which the Russian Government began to enforce the operation of new discriminatory edicts against the Jews.

1827 Introduction of military service for Jewish youth (cantonists). Service was for twenty five years.

1835 Official establishment of the Pale of Settlement and the Regulations on Jewish Affairs, restricting even more severely Jewish freedom of movement and preventing settlement outside very restricted geographical areas.

1844 Dissolution of the *Kehillot*.

1846 Visit by Sir Moses Montefiore to Vilnius and Kaunas en route for St Petersburg. On leaving he declared to the leaders of the community: "I leave you but my heart will ever remain with you. When my brethren suffer, I feel it painfully: when the have reason to weep my eyes shed tears."

1855 With the death of Nicholas I and accession of Alexander II the Cantonist system is abolished.

1858 Partial permission for Jews to leave the Pales and live elsewhere in Russia.

1867 The Great Famine, which led to the outbreak of cholera and the beginnings of a mass emigration.

1872 First Jewish public Library in Lithuania founded in Vilnius.

1881 Assassination of Alexander II and accession of Alexander III. Outbreak of pogroms in Southern Russia and the beginning of the flight of Jews en masse to the West.

1881-97 Emigration of over 50,000 Jews from Kaunas.

1882 Introduction in May of the Provisional Laws, restricting Jewish rights of settlement, of ownership of land, and of permission to trade on Sundays.

1886 First Jewish Labour societies founded in Vilnius.

1891 A new "Great Famine" and more pogroms in the south.

1893 Foundation of Mizrachi in Bialystock.

1897 The Bund (General Jewish Workers' Union) founded in Vilnius. Opposes Zionism and the use of Hebrew. General Census shows 755,000 Jews in Lithuania (212,600 in Kaunas).

1897-1914 Emigration of 33,800 Jews from Kaunas.

1903 Theodore Herzl, the founder of Zionism, came to Vilnius. Mass demonstrations in support, which the Russian troops dispersed by force. He wrote "Yesterday, Vilna day, was something I shall never forget".

1906 Following 1905 revolution, first Duma is established; Naftali Fridman elected from Kaunas specifically as a Jew. Prohibition of political organisations "with foreign connections" – i.e. Zionists.

1915 In April and May the Russian Government ordered the expulsion of all Jews from Lithuania, on the alleged grounds that they were helping the German invaders. More than 120,000 have to leave. In September Lithuania was occupied by the German army.

1917 February Revolution. Overthrow of the Tsar in St Petersburg. A liberal, provisional government is formed. Then, in October, the Bolsheviks mount a coup.

1918 Lithuania declares independence.

1919 Recognition of Lithuania. (August) Paris Declaration gives official – but short-lived – autonomy to the Jewish communities in Lithuania.

1920 Seizure by Poland of Vilnius; Kaunas the new capital of Lithuania. Foundation of Yiddish Reali Gymnasium in Vilkomir.

1923 The last National Jewish Assembly, held in Kaunas.

1923 National census shows Jewish population of 154,000.

1924 The Festivals Law prohibits working on Sundays and other Christian festivals.

1926 Military coup d'état; end of democracy in Lithuania.

1939 January: German-Lithuanian non-aggression pact; March: German occupation of Memel. September: Soviet occupation of Vilnius; October: Russian-Lithuanian mutual assistance agreement. Vilnius restored to Lithuania.

1940 Soviet occupation of Lithuania.

1941 June: Soviet deportation of 30,000 "enemies of the State" including a large number of Jews who were by this means saved from subsequent murder by the Nazis. Germany attacks Soviet Union. June 24th: German occupation of Kaunas and Vilnius. Massacre in Kaunas by Lithuanian partisans of 4,000 Jews; August: Lithuania, Estonia, and Latvia incorporated by the German administration into Ostland. Establishment of Ghettos in Kaunas, Vilnius, and Siauliai. Election of Dr Elhanan Elkes as head of the Kaunas Ghetto. September: Appointment of Jacob Gens as head of the Jewish police in Vilnius. October 28th: "Di groyse aktie" – the murder of about 11,000 Kaunas Jews in Fort Nine. Between June and November 1941 the vast majority (about 200,000 out of an estimated 220,000 Lithuanian Jews had been murdered.

1942 February seizure of 100,000 books for despatch to Germany.

1943 September: Liquidation of Vilnius Ghetto November. The Murder of the Children (Kinderaktion) in Siauliai. July: Deportation of Jews from Kaunas to the concentration camps at Stutthof (women) and Dachau (men). July 14th: Entry of Red Army into Lithuania.

1944 Approximately 10,000 Jews in Lithuania survive the German occupation.

1948-53 Anti-Semitism in Lithuania consolidates; Jews under increasing pressure and growing antagonism. Jewish schools and institutions closed down.

1979-98 Jewish population fell from 23,562 to 4,500.

1990 Lithuanian Independence from Soviet control internationally recognised. Declaration by the President of Lithuania condemning the role of Lithuanian anti-Semites against the Jews of Lithuania.[1]

"The fates of Lithuanian Jews are varied. Some of us have survived. Some of us were from elsewhere. But everyone of us are from the vanished *shtetlach* – the towns and villages which had Jews."

Rosa Belioskiene, chief curator
of the Vilna Gaon Jewish State Museum.

List of towns

List of Lithuanian towns visited, with Yiddish names in brackets

Darbenai (Dorbian)
Kaunas (Kovno)
Kedainiai (Keidan)
Kernave (Kernava)
Kretinga (Ketingan)
Kurkliai (Kurkli)
Laukuva (Loykuva)
Laukzeme (Loykzim)
Liubavas (Lubow)
Luoke (Luknik)
Nemencine (Nemenchin)
Paberze (Podberezhe)
Pakruojis (Pokroi)
Palanga (Polangen)
Paneriai (Ponary)
Plateliai (Plotel)
Plokstine (Plokstine)
Plunge (Plungian)
Raseiniai (Rasein)
Rietavas (Riteve)
Skuodas (Skud)
Slobodka (Vilijampole)
Telsiai (Telz)
Trakai (Troki)
Ukmerge (Vilkomir)
Vaitimenai (Vaitumen)
Vilnius (Vilna)
Ziezmariai (Zhezmir)

Darbenai (Dorbian)
Dorbian is near Lake Derba, in the Kretinga district. The community developed in the early 19th century and in 1897 Dorbian had a population of about 1,130 Jews out of a total of about 1500. By 1940, however, the number of Jews had fallen to about 800 out of a total of some 2,000. The synagogue was destroyed by fire in 1909 and never rebuilt. The Jews owned several small factories in this shtetl, including a factory for soft drinks. There was a sawmill, also owned by a Jewish family. There is a well-maintained Jewish cemetery here.

Kaunas (Kovno)
There have been Jews in Kaunas since the 15th century, although at times they were persecuted by the city authorities and forced to find refuge in the neighbouring community of Slobodka. Although theoretically a distinct community, in many ways Slobodka acted as a suburb of Kaunas. Relations between the Jewish and non-Jewish inhabitants of the city continued to be bad throughout the 18th century, and it was not until the early 19th century that the Jews could be considered as having finally established themselves there.

Kedainiai (Keidan)
Kedainiai is about 30 miles north of Kovno. It has a long history as a centre for Jewish economic and social life in Lithuania, going back to the 15th century. At the beginning of the 18th century the community had for a time fallen into poverty and the community authorities were unable to repay a debt to the local squire who on a Sabbath morning sealed the doors of the synagogue while the community was at prayer and refused to release them until the debt was paid. The town, however, gradually recovered, and even attained prosperity during the 19th century when there was a substantial Russian garrison in the town and the railway line between Libau and Rumania passed nearby. The 1890s saw a change, and in 1897 there were 3,733 Jews out of a total population of about 6,000. During the First World War the Jews were expelled to Russia but afterwards they returned, and in 1923 there were 2,500 Jews out of a total of about 7,500. One of the occupations of the Jews of Keidan was the growing of cucumbers, which was virtually a Jewish monopoly.

Kurkliai (Kurkli)
Kurkliai is in the Ukmerge/Vilkomir district. In the years before the German invasion of Lithuania there was a Jewish population of about 250. As elsewhere in Lithuania many Jewish inhabitants had earlier emigrated, to South Africa and the USA. In the 19th century there had been two prayer houses in the town; one with a stove used in the winter while the other, 'the new shul', was used in the summer. Eventually, when the older building seemed about to collapse, the stove was moved to the newer one.

Laukuva (Loykuva)
Loykuva is in the Tavrig district, near Ritova and between Kovno and Memel. In 1897 there were 418 Jews here, nearly half of the total population. Many emigrated to South Africa, America or Palestine, but on the eve of the Holocaust there were still 450 Jews remaining. Chapeltown Hebrew Congregation, in Leeds, West Yorkshire, also known as Chapeltown United Synagogue, was originally known, in 1888, as the Lowkever Synagogue – the town from where most of its original congregants originated.

Laukzeme (Loykzim)
Laukzeme is in the Kretinga district, north of Dorbian, and had a Jewish community until in the mid-19th century the local landlord expelled his Jews. Many moved to Dorbian.

Luoke (Luknik)
Luknik is in the Telz district, and there had been Jews there in the middle of the 18th century; in 1766 there were 566 Jews. In 1897 there were 798 Jews, nearly half of the total population, but by 1939 there were only 100 Jewish families. This town no longer has any Jews living there. There is still a cemetery with some 200 stones.

Palanga (Polangen)
The site of a Jewish community as early as the 15th century and there were 398 Jews there in 1765. By 1887 there were 1,100 Jews, but by 1939 Palanga had fewer than 700. One of the most important industries was the manufacture of amber jewellery; there were dozens of factories in which nearly all of the workers were Jewish. The town was also a popular holiday resort for many Lithuanians.

Plateliai (Plotel)
Plateliai is in the Kretinga district. The community declined from 171 Jews in 897 to eighteen Jewish families in 1939. The decline was largely a result of emigration to America and South Africa, but was affected also by the expulsion of the Jews in 1915 during the First World War and the destruction by fire of half the town in 1923.

Plokstine (Plokstine)
There is a former Soviet nuclear missile base located at Plokstine, deep in the woods of Zemaitija National Park. It is located to the south east of Lake Plateliai. It is now a tourist attraction.

Plunge (Plungian)
Plunge, seven miles from the German border and in the Telz District, had a substantial Jewish community at the census of 1897; there were then 2,502 Jews, over half of the general population. However, as a result of increasing economic discrimination against Jewish enterprises by 1939, the jewish population had fallen to 1,700. Many of the Jews emigrated to South Africa. There was still, however, a very active Jewish political and cultural life.

Raseiniai (Rasein)
This was one of the first Jewish communities to be established in Lithuania. Just as Vilna had a reputation for Talmudic learning so did Rasein. It was known as "The Jerusalem of Zamut". In 1842 the majority of the population of 7,455 were Jewish and by 1897 the Jewish population had reached 9,000 (90 per cent of the total). There were ten synagogues in 1929. But the Jewish community dwindled to 2,000 by 1939. There was an active Zionist movement and an impressive list of charities. Listed among them were The Union for the Aid of Poor Mothers and Hospitality for Travellers.

Rietavas (Riteve)
In the district of Telz, the nearest train station being in Plunge. The land in the town belonged to the Aginsky family, the first head of which made himself thoroughly hated by the Jews, who on his death instituted a special form of Purim celebration. One of his actions was to take over the Beit Hamidresh, the religious study centre of the community, and change it into a pigsty. In 1897 there were nearly 1,400 Jews in Rietavos, some 80 per cent of the total population.

Skuodas (Skud)
Skuodas was In the Kretinga district, and was the centre of a group of flourishing Jewish communities. In 1847 there were over 1,800 Jews there; in 1897 2,292; and in 1921 it had 3,853. In 1939 there were still over 2,500 Jews there, about half of the general population. The Jews worked in trade, agriculture, industry, and crafts. Skud had two cities, the Old City and the New City. The Jewish cemetery was near the Old City, and it was divided up into three sections: the old part for the rich and distinguished; the new part was for the poor – and the middle section was. The preserve of the middle class.

Slobodka (Vilijampole)
Slobodka, in the Kovno district, was largely regarded as a suburb of Kaunas although it was independently founded, and had a reputation for piety. The first leader and founder of the Musar movement, Rabbi Israel Salanter (1810-1883) had set up a yeshiva in Kovno. Later the yeshiva moved to Slobodka. Usually, any move of Jews from Kovno to Slobodka signified controversy or expulsion of some kind. Musar, literally "moral instruction", combined the Vilna Gaon's emphasis on learning of religious texts with involvement in the wider community. The movement may have had opponents in Kovno (and Vilna), but it became popular outside of Lithuania – in Israel, the United States and Great Britain.

Telsiai (Telz)
Telz, near Plungian and the capital of the Telz district, is one of the oldest cities in Lithuania. In 1897 it had a Jewish population of 3,088, over half of the total population. The Jews were expelled during the First World War but returned afterwards, and by 1939 there were 2,800 Jews out of a total population of 8,000. Many Jews were engaged in trade, in produce, in woods, and in crafts, but a major source of income came from the great Telz Yeshiva (1875 – 1941), amongst the largest and most famous in Lithuania. One can still see the yeshiva building and the synagogue, and the streets of the "Old Town" where the former Jewish houses and shops still stand. One of the great personalities of the community was the secular poet Yehuda Leib Gordon. Few Jewish families remain.

Trakai (Troki)
For centuries Trakai was the centre of Karaite Jews in Lithuania. The people of this branch of Karaism are direct descendants of some 400 Karaites Turkic warriors who were invited into Lithuania in 1397 by Grand Duke Vytauatas to be his personal bodyguards. They speak a Turkic-based language and use the Hebrew alphabet. The Karaites believe in the Torah, the Old Testament, but reject rabbinical authority. At one time mainstream Orthodox Jews were forbidden to settle in Trakai. But by 1897 there were over 800 "rabbinic" Jews in the town. In Lithuania the Karaites are officially regarded as a distinct ethnic group. The Nazis also treated them differently and spared them. There are up to 100 Karaites living in Trakai today. Most Karaite Jews, descendants of other branches of the sect, now live in Israel.

Ukmerge (Vilkomir)
The capital of the Ukmerge district, Ukmerge was on the frontier between the Poles, the crusading Teutonic knights and the Russians, and eventually developed into an important trade and administrative centre. During the 19th century it was hit by plagues, famine and fires, and indeed in 1878 the whole city was burned down. Jewish communities all over Lithuania donated money for its rebuilding and donations were received from the Rothschild and Montefiore families. Although the city's importance as a trade centre was affected by the building of the railway line from Libau to Rumania, its Jewish population maintained its importance and numbers. In 1864 it had 4,561 Jews and in 1897 it had 7,287 Jews, over half of the total population. In 1935 it had a Jewish population of over 8,000. It was a centre of a strong "haredi" orthodox tradition, and there was also a very active Zionist presence before the annexation by the Soviet Union in 1940, when religious and nationalistic Jewish life was systematically destroyed – even before the arrival of the Germans.

Zeizmariai (Zhezmir)
Zhezmir is in the Troke district, some 20 miles from Kovno. In 1766 there were nearly 500 Jews living there, but the population declined (largely due to emigration) and by 1941 there were only 200 families left. The town suffered a number of natural disasters; in 1918 most of the town, including three prayer houses, burned down, and there was another fire in 1923. But it managed to maintain an orphanage, a library, and a branch of the Jewish People's Bank.

Map of Lithuania

Vilnius
(Vilna)

Jewish Street – or Zydu in Lithuanian – cuts through the heart of old town Vilnius, or Vilna, as it was known to the Yiddish-speaking Jews. But there's not much overtly Jewish about it anymore. The Great Synagogue, which once stood at the end of Jewish Street was dynamited by the Nazis and then later bulldozed by the Soviets; there's now a Soviet-built kindergarten and basketball court where the synagogue used to stand.

Yet, for centuries old Vilna had been a centre of Jewish culture. Jews had lived there from the first half of the 16th century, and according to one tradition there was a synagogue founded as early as 1573. In 1645 a census conducted by the municipality revealed 262 Jewish families and a total Jewish population of close to 3,000 people. From that time onwards there had been a strong tradition of learning and this reached a peak during the lifetime of the Vilna Gaon in the 18th century. Vilna became the centre of Jewish printing in Lithuania, and the printing house of Romm (which produced the first Vilna Talmud) had for nearly a hundred years a monopoly on Hebrew printing in Russia.

Vilna was the archetypal Lithuanian Jewish community and indeed was commonly known as the Jerusalem of Lithuania or the Jerusalem of the North. During the 19th century the town had an elaborate educational system with a number of Jewish schools teaching practical skills. It was a centre of acute controversy over Zionism and also a centre of left-wing Jewish revolutionary movements. The opposition to Zionism came in part from the religious right of which Rabbi Hayyim Grodzinski was one of the prominent leaders. Vilna was also the founding centre of the Bund, set up in 1897, a manifestation of the growing Jewish labour movement in Jewish Lithuania. The result of this diverse activity was that there were Jewish schools that were anti-Zionist and taught in Hebrew, pro-Zionist schools that taught in Yiddish, and others that taught in Russian. Jewish publishing houses were producing more than a dozen Yiddish newspapers, together with many magazines and books.

After the First World War Vilna became a centre of contention between Poland and Lithuania. It had originally been allocated to Lithuania, but the Polish government argued that there was not a majority of Lithuanian inhabitants and seized possession. In fact the Poles were partially right for it had a population of over 200,000 of whom 80,000 were Jews, 60,000 Poles, and 60,000 Lithuanians and other nationalities. The Jews in Vilna had their own educational system, and the predominant vehicle was the Tarbut (Culture) movement, which was neither religious nor anti-religious but rather strongly Zionist.

Most outward signs of the 600-year Jewish presence in this city were obliterated as a consequence of the devastating 1941- 1944 German occupation – such as the noted Yiddish Institute of Higher Learning (YIVO) and the Strashum Library, which housed the world's largest collection of Yiddish-language books; both were destroyed by the Nazis.

The Jewish ghetto was encircled by barbed wire and transformed into a prison camp for the city's 60,000 Jews, nearly all of whom were later marched to the Paneriai (Ponary) forest eight kilometres away and executed.

While it is true that few traces of the city's rich Jewish past survived the war, save for a few commemorative plaques (one is on Stikliu and another on Rudninku in the old city), there are ambitious plans for a Jewish revival of sorts. The legislature recently voted to restore and, in some cases, entirely rebuild scores of Jewish landmarks.

The government is footing part of the bill, and a Jewish Cultural Fund was created to seek private donations for the project. Emanuelis Zingeris, a recent parliamentarian and chairman of the fund, said the restoration will be a fitting memorial. "We don't need another cemetery marker," he said. "We need a monument, not to how Jews died, but to how they lived. That's what this will be."

Easier tasks, like repainting Hebrew letters that once graced Jewish storefronts, have already begun. Rebuilding the cathedral-sized Great Synagogue, once the focal point of Vilnius Jewish life, will be harder – and far more costly: building the 3,000-square-metre synagogue from scratch will cost some ten million dollars. The reconstruction of some thirty buildings in what are now parks and abandoned lots will cost some ninety million dollars more. "This restoration will be something Lithuanian parents can show their kids and say, 'Look here, this is our heritage. Great people once lived here,'" said Zingeris. "We need to bring this Jewishness back into the circulation of Lithuanian culture."

Vilnius's Jewish past inevitably draws tens of thousands of Jewish visitors a year from the United States, Israel, Argentina and also South Africa, where as many as eighty percent of the nation's 90,000 Jews are descended from Lithuanian Jews.[2]

The Vilna Gaon

Elijah ben Solomon Zalman (1720-1797), known as the Vilna Gaon, is the most renowned of all Lithuania's rabbis. He wrote works in all spheres of Jewish scholarship: commentaries on the Bible, Hebrew grammar, kabbalah and biblical geography. The Gaon's greatest achievement was his editing and commentary on the Babylonian Talmud. But he is equally remembered for his opposition to the mystical Hassidic movement and the Hassidic rebbes who rejected the importance of rabbinic learning. He was also opposed to the Haskalah movement of Enlightenment led by Moses Mendelssohn of Berlin. His influence remains alive today among the small remaining Jewish community in Vilnius. He has become an iconic figure. In 1997, at the 200th anniversary commemoration of his death, the president of Lithuania spoke about the Vilna Gaon as a symbol for Jewish-Christian reconciliation.[3]

[1] The Vilna Gaon's grave in Vilnius Cemetery, 2002.
His bones were moved from the old Jewish cemetery at Shnipishok to the Jewish cemetery at Saltonishkiu after the war. As I was drawing I heard a man hear singing Yiskor most beautifully – the memorial prayer. He then asked me for money!

[2] Old street, Vilnius – with arch, 2002.

**[3]
Oldest synagogue in Vilnius, 6 Guilu St., 2002.**
In the centre of old Vilnius. The oldest part of the synagogue is 300 years old. But it is a sad place. A Star of David is daubed on the front. It is falling apart inside. Rubbish strewn everywhere. People are suspicious of me and tell me to go away.

**[4]
Oldest synagogue in Vilnius – side view, 2002.**

Lithuanian Synagogues

There were a vast number of different kinds of synagogues in Lithuania before the Second World War – in Vilnius alone there were thought to be around 100 places of worship – some were so informally organised that the true numbers could never be known. The number, size and appearance of prayer houses were determined by the number of Jewish houses, the needs of the community and its financial capabilities. Often houses of prayer were built as multifaceted sets of buildings, divided by season (summer and winter synagogues), and by belonging to a particular social standing (merchants, labourers) or occupation (musicians, tailors, etc).

Synagogues did not dominate in the panoramas of towns and cities due to prohibitions imposed as early as the 17th century. They had to be lower than churches and had to stand at a certain distance from them.

The specific nature and shape of synagogues was dictated by functional demands, with divisions into male and female sides. In one-storey synagogues women prayed on the right-hand side, and in buildings with upper floors, on one or three sides of the galleries.

The Ark, where the Torah scrolls are kept, is always located at the eastern wall so the worshipper is facing Jerusalem. The Bima, the platform for the reading of the Torah, is usually situated in the central part of the hall.

Most Lithuanian synagogues did not survive the Second World War. The Great Synagogue in Vilnius, built in the Renaissance period and later reconstructed was damaged during the war and then completely destroyed by the Soviets in 1955-1957 when Vilnius was being reconstructed. It is said that in its pomp it had room for up to 4,000 congregants, with standing room only on the High Holy Days. Many other synagogues were bulldozed after the war; still others were severely damaged by being turned into warehouses, manufacturing shops, gyms, etc. Many others lie derelict.[4]

[5] Locked in Choral Synagogue, Vilnius, 2002.
I was locked in the synagogue for two hours. No escape. They did it to prevent vandals coming in. It is the only functioning synagogue in Vilnius. Before the war there were around a hundred synagogues or *shteebls*, smaller prayer communities, holding services.

[6] Choral Synagogue, Vilnius – entrance, 2002.
A small community gathered for the evening service, enough to make a minyan, a prayer quorum, of ten men. The facade bears an inscription in Hebrew: A house of prayer is a holy place for all peoples.

[7] Inside corridor of Choral Synagogue, 2003.
Here the Jews with maybe more money worshipped. Opulent. But not as opulent as it might have been. The original design included three domes but the synagogue board opted for a simpler, less costly design.

[8] Ghetto of Vilnius, House, 10 Rudnuha, 2003.
Originally the Road of Nobles, became Jewish at the end of the 18th century. My guide, Rosa Bielioskiene, the chief curator of the Vilna Gaon Jewish Museum, was born here. It was used as a workshop when the ghetto was established. Jews were put in this big square when the Nazis came, then herded off to the station nearby and on to the camps.

[9] Synagogue – back entrance, Pilymo Street, Vilnius, 2002.
Another synagogue, virtually derelict. It was falling down, in a dilapidated state, being used as a storehouse. It has a large courtyard, a backyard. Typical shape of synagogue windows in Lithuania.

How to recognise a Jewish home

Rosa Bielioiskiene, chief curator of the Vilna Gaon Jewish State Museum explained to me that usually there would be no front garden. While their Christian neighbours had flowers in their front gardens those Jewish homes with gardens would be filled with vegetables. Before the First World War plots of land would not be sold to non-Lithuanians and flowers would have been wasteful. Most Jews would rent the gardens and plant vegetables by the side or at the back of the house. Between the wars, when Lithuania became independent, Jews became citizens and obtained equal rights.

Russian Tsarist laws included taxation in accordance with how many windows were in the property. It is thought a window tax meant Jews paid more than anyone else. So one often finds Jewish homes where windows have been built or rebuilt next to each other to count as one window and thereby avoid taxes.

Houses and shops on street corners of two streets were often cut back so the entrance would be put on the corner to make the places visible from both streets and thereby help business. If there was trouble, maybe this also helped the Jews escape more easily.

[10]
Jewish homes behind synagogue in Pilymo Street, Vilnius, 2002.

[11]
Jewish home behind synagogue in Pilymo Street, Vilnius, 2002.
The house is empty. A cat jumps out of the window … in the same courtyard as the old synagogue.

[12] Woman carrying sack, Vilnius, 2002.
She was standing inside a church within the compound of Vilnius University holding her sack, listening to classical music streaming out from the university. She was mesmerised. She stood there oblivious for half an hour.

[13] St Casimir's Church. Built 1604, Vilnius, 2002.
My first day in Vilnius. I was sitting in a café, my companions were speaking in Lithuanian, and, somewhat bored I started to look at the church and to draw. It seemed magical, beautiful.

[14]
Jewish Museum bannisters – was Hebrew School, Vilnius, 2002.
A Jewish school opened here in 1928 for 10-16 year-olds in part of a large private house with ballrooms. Old people remember sliding down the bannisters. Closed by the Russians in 1940. Given back to the Jewish community in 1991.

[15]
Back of Hebrew School/Jewish Museum. View from office, Vilnius, 2004.
Drawn from the window of the office in the Jewish Museum.

[16]
Looking out of Jewish Museum, Vilnius, 2002.
Eerie feeling when I started painting. The Nazis put Jews from Belarus into the courtyard before sending them to the local ghettos. Did the schoolchildren flee from there to the balcony in a vain attempt to escape?

[17] **Homes next to Vilna Gaon's house, with statue, Vilnius, 2002.**
Where the Vilna Gaon lived is now an empty piece of ground next to his statue.
The area is adorned by plaster-and-brick buildings, beautifully restored.

[18] Zemaitijos Street, Vilnius, 2003.
I sat there watching while washing was being put on lines. Cats were ambling around. Old people sat outside, just looking. No one was the least bit interested in me, a small woman sitting on a stool, just looking and drawing.

[19] Mother and two children, Zeizmariai, 2004.
They were unaware of the mezuzah still on door. It has been painted over.
They all lived in one room and a kitchen; had been a Jewish home.

[20]
Woman cleaning window, Uzipos, Vilnius, 2004.

[21]
Houses and synagogue in Uzipos, with alterations, Vilnius, 2004.
Very cold. I couldn't feel my hands. What was a synagogue, on the right, has been built over with a staircase which obscures the windows. It is now an artists' area – home to painters, writers and young musicians.

[22] **Synagogue in Uzipos, Vilnius, 2004.**
I sit here all alone finding Jewish house after Jewish house.
Too much to draw and I am getting so cold.

[23] Courtyard of Choral Synagogue, Vilnius, 2003.
There used to be a succah on the balcony, a temporary dwelling without a proper roof, decorated with fruit and leaves to celebrate the festival of Sukkoth.

[24] 100th **Anniversary celebrations in Choral Synagogue, Vilnius, 2003.**
Important Israeli rabbis and local dignitaries were there. They tried to make it special but it was very amateurish. They lit torches and walked round the shul. Men downstairs, women upstairs.

[25] Choral Synagogue, Vilnius, 2004.

Europas Parkas

"We are fascinated by the way you create and are pleased to invite you to the Europas Parkas. We will be glad to assist you in exploring Lithuanian culture and traditions as well as capturing remnants of Jewish buildings"

Gintaras Karosas, president of Europas Parkas,
Open Air Museum of the Centre of Europe
15 December 2001 in a letter to Naomi Alexander.

The Europas Parkas is a museum set in nature with more than ninety outdoor exhibits created by artists from around the world. Naomi Alexander was one of its first artists-in-residence there who was a painter. The goal of the museum is to give artistic significance to Lithuania's location as the geographic centre of the European continent, and to present the best of Lithuanian and international modern art. Among the exhibits are works by Magdalena Abakonovicz, Sol LeWitt and Dennis Oppenheim.

[26]
Europas Parkas – stone sculpture (1), 2002.
I am looking towards the rocks of Magdalena Abakanowicz's sculpture Space of Unknown Growth. I feel alone but happy and peaceful, imbibing the solitude and my family history. My grandmother came from Lithuania; I see her everywhere, Freda Selig.

[27]
Europas Parkas – stone sculpture (2), 2002.

[28]
Europas Parkas – outside the restaurant, 2002.

[29]
Lake and swimmers at the Green Lakes near Europas Parkas, 2002.
Did my ancestors swim in these lakes? I swam there, near the River Neris. 15 miles north of Vilnius.

[30]
Europas Parkas – house where I lived, 2002.
House where I lived at Europas Parkas. Locked here for months, but so beautiful.

[31]
Farmstead. Man with scythe near Europas Parkas, Skirgiskes, 2002.
When I first came to Lithuania, in 2002, I saw plenty of scythes and ploughs and very few tractors. But it is slowly changing.

Liubavas

[32] The mill house near Europas Parkas, 2003.

Jews and non-Jews lived side by side in the shtetls of Lithuania. Jews roamed the farms and villages selling their wares. Even today one can see how people lived; the harsh, grinding poverty in the villages, the scattered homesteads and array of farms and the fine houses – and all around are forests, lakes and vast open spaces.

[33] House in Liubavas. Owner was sent to Siberia, near Europas Parkas. 2003.
House of Jewish man sent to Siberia by the Soviets. Drawn to it by the peaceful location and the mystery of the man whose fate is unknown.

[34] Woman resting after potato pickings near Europas Parkas, 2003.

[35] Woman doing washing, Liubavas, 2002.

[36] **Disabled woman outside house next to pond, Liubavas, 2002.**
As I walked around the lodge on a beautiful day, the disabled woman with the Zimmer frame slowly walked around, enabling me to sketch her in several poses. The sun was shining, butterflies everywhere. I felt at peace.

[37] Europas Parkas – lost in woods, 2003.
Getting lost in these woods I began to panic. So easy to get lost. I was collecting mushrooms – beautiful big bolete.

[38]
House in Liubavas, 2002.
You would be unlikely to find an old house in this area owned by Jews.

[39]
Old chapel, Liubavas, 2002.

[40]
Home of elderly lady, Liubavas, 2002.
A friendly old lady who lived there gave me a drink of a pink coloured juice. I was afiraid it was from the well and I might get ill. She stood over me as I drank it.

[41]
Little girl and house, Liubavas, 2002.
This is the place that no ghosts rise – only butterflies.

Kernave

[42]
A soldier folds his arm at the fair at Kernave, 2002.
6 July is King Mindaugus's Day, a public holiday. A day for pagans and nationalists. Locals are celebrating the festival by barbecuing a pig at a fete, and getting very drunk. Mindaugus was a Christian who united Lithuania's pagan tribal duchies. Crowned by order of Pope Innocentius 1V in 1253 but later overthrown and the country returned to paganism for more than a century. Kernave hosts the Stonehenge of Lithuania: a UNESCO World Heritage Site famed for its ancient Stone Age, pre-Christian hill forts.

[43]
Fair at Kernave, 2002.
"The Lithuanians are proud of their heritage and will tell you how they were among the last pagans in Europe. The peasants maintained their unique culture and language under centuries of oppression and of the grand dukes who established a brief empire; their names will roll off the tongue: Mindaugas, Gediminas, Vytautas …" – Betty Birsky.[5]

[44] A non-Jewish home, Kernave, 2002.
There were some isolated farmsteads.

Trakai
(Troki)

For centuries Trakai was the centre of Karaite Jews in Lithuania. The people of this branch of Karaism are direct descendants of some 400 Karaites Turkic warriors who were invited into Lithuania in 1397 by Grand Duke Vytauatas to be his personal bodyguards. They speak a Turkic-based language and use the Hebrew alphabet. The Karaites believe in the Torah, the Old Testament, but reject rabbinical authority. At one time mainstream Orthodox Jews were forbidden to settle in Trakai. But by 1897 there were over 800 "rabbinic" Jews in the town. In Lithuania the Karaites are officially regarded as a distinct ethnic group. The Nazis also treated them differently and spared them. There are up to 100 Karaites living in Trakai today. Most Karaite Jews, descendants of other branches of the sect, now live in Israel.

[45]
Chickens next to old church near Trakai, 2002.

[46]
Church near Trakai, 2002.
Close to where the Karaites live.

[47] **Karaite house of prayer, Trakai, 2002.**
Karaite house of worship They light Friday night candles, have two challahs, don't intermarry and do not eat pork. The women are separated from the men, upstairs as in Orthodox synagogues. One Karaite member told me, adamantly, he wasn't Jewish. For when the Nazis came they measured the noses of his mother and father and said they were not Jewish.

[48] Exterior of Karaite prayer house, Trakai, 2002.

Nemencine

[49] **Old house in Nemencine, 2003.**
I can imagine a poor Jew living here and the last inhabitants being led away to be shot. A young couple were there; they came out and stared at me, mistrustful. Just next to the river.

[50] Church in Nemencine, near Europas Parkas, 2003.
Nearest village to Europas Parkas on the River Neris. Had a small Jewish community pre-war. I had just watched the priest emerging with his congregation and I thought of the long-lost Jews who had roamed nearby. The church would have dominated the shtetl.

[51] Two women with pails, Nemencine, 2003.
They couldn't read and were shy. They were getting water from the pump. They couldn't read my letter of introduction in Lithuanian and they couldn't read Russian either. I guess they couldn't read at all. They shook their heads and their fingers in turn.

[52] Woman with horse and cow, Nemencine, 2004.

Paberze

[53] Building, Glitiskes near Paberze, 2002.
Was it a synagogue? But a porch has been added and larger buildings. By 1923 there was only one Jew living there. My life was threatened here. An Arab invited me to a circumcision coming-of-age party, I was welcomed in by some fifty men for a brandy. Then he crossed his throat with his finger and said: "Then I will do this to you."

Ukmerge

[54]
Ukmerge Synagogue, 2003.

Rietavas

[55]
Rietavas Synagogue, 2004.
At one time the land in the town belonged to the Aginsky family, the first head of which made himself thoroughly hated by the Jews by taking over the Beit Hamedresh of the community – the study house of one of the synagogues – and changing it into a pigsty. On his death the Jews instituted a special form of Purim celebration. In 1897 there were nearly 1,400 Jews, some eighty per cent of the total population.

Kedainiai
(Keidan)

Kedainiai is about thirty miles north of Kovno. It has a long history as a centre for Jewish economic and social life in Lithuania, going back to the 15th century. At the beginning of the 18th century the community had for a time fallen into poverty and the community authorities ed to the local squire who on a Sabbath morning sealed the doors of the synagogue while the community was at prayer and refused to release them until the debt was paid. The town, however, gradually recovered, and even attained prosperity during the 19th century when there was a substantial Russian garrison in the town and the railway line between Libau and Rumania passed nearby. The 1890s saw a change, and in 1897 there were 3,733 Jews out of a total population of about 6,000. During the First World War the Jews were expelled to Russia but afterwards they returned, and in 1923 there were 2,500 Jews out of a total of about 7,500. One of the occupations of the Jews of Keidan was the growing of cucumbers, which was virtually a Jewish monopoly.

[56] Doors of collapsing old house, Jew Street, Kedainiai, 2004.
Zhyder Street means Jewish Street – Zhyd being a contemptuous term for a Jew. Dovydas Leibzonas, a survivor of the Kovno ghetto, took me to Kedainiai and told me his story of survival.

[57] Mustard house in Zydu Street, Kedainiai, 2004.
It was a pretty house in Kedainiai. Zydu. (Jew) Street.

[58]
Two synagogues, Kedainiai, 2004.
Now in private hands. A beautiful day in the very clean, large shtetl; architecture very beautiful and Dutch-looking. There was once another building in front of these two. Smoke from factory chimneys on the outskirts is now polluting the town and everyone wants to leave.

"Members of the shul and the *kloyz* (a smaller version of a shul), the two main groups, were always at each others throats. Each had its own rabbi, and each tried to dominate community affairs. There were two separate Passover charity drives. And nobody would let a baker of the other faction bake matzos for him until his oven had been purified and certified kosher by a neutral party. … Once the kloyz rabbi, the late Reb Berl Mazik, announced that Jews were absolutely forbidden to carry anything on Sabbath, while the rabbi of the shul said otherwise. Comical it was to see young boys from the shul group, carrying tsholents for the kloyzner families. Only in the cemetery did harmony prevail."

Chaim Yaakov Epstein[6]

Brick Ovens

"Heating of the houses was by means of brick ovens lined on the outside with white or brown tiles. These ovens, which reached almost to the ceiling, made quite an attractive appearance, but were deficient as heating media. Too much of the heat went out the chimney. The fuel most commonly used was peat, which is a highly organic soil of partially decomposed matter. It was mined in the numerous peat bogs in the area. The water was drained off and the solid matter was put in moulds of a uniform size and allowed to dry in the sun. The dried, rectangular-shaped bricks were sold at three-and-a-half to five rubles a thousand. Generally twenty bricks were used at a time. Since only about half of the peat was combustible, fresh fires had to be built often, after removal of ashes and other non-combustible matter. It was not a very dependable source of heat, but it had the advantage of being cheap. Cooking was done in a fireplace, which generally formed an extension of the front part of the oven. The pot was put on a tripod underneath, which was built on a wood fire."

From the autobiography of the late Jacob Hyam Rubenstein[7]

[59] "Jewish" oven, Dorbian, 2004.

[60] Oven, Zeizmariai, 2002.
A typical tiled brick oven. People would sleep on top to keep warm. Had a cup of tea outside with the couple who lived there who showed me their outside toilet so I could photograph it. They had electricity and a TV in the bedroom.

[61]
Woman by oven, in house in Jewish district, Slobodka, Kaunas, 2004.

[62]
Oven, Dorbian, 2002.
This was the home of the keeper of the new Jewish cemetery in Dorbian.

[63]
Woman in room, Slobodka, Kaunas, 2004.
Her father built the oven after a Jewish dentist had left. She had been there since the war ended. The front of the oven is in the kitchen and the back of it, as can be seen, opens up into the sitting room.

[64]
Woman in kitchen, Slobodka, Kaunas, 2004.
Here you can see the same woman in her kitchen and the remaining brick oven can be seen.

[65]
Pakruojis Synagogue, 2003.
One of only eight known remaining wooden synagogues in Lithuania. A Soviet feel to the area, but some lovely old Jewish homes remain. The shul was located behind apartment blocks near a running stream. I peered in to look through the holes in the wooden building. It was a shambles inside. Then I felt an arm around me. It was a drunk who wouldn't leave me alone.

Wooden synagogues

The wooden synagogues of Lithuania are rotting away. Today, there are only eight wooden synagogues (of hundreds) still standing in the remote villages of Pakruojis, Tirksliai, Seda, Zeizmariai, Kurkliai, Alanta, Rozalimas and Kaltinenai.

One of the first buildings constructed in each new shtetl was the synagogue. The oldest of these baroque buildings (dating from the 17th century) were scattered in villages across the country like Valkininkai, Jubarkas, Saukenai and Vilkaviskis. These villages once had sizable Jewish populations and in some cases were completely Jewish. Construction of wooden synagogues continued until the early part of the 20th century, with more than twenty three constructed between the 19th and early 20th centuries.

Generally, wooden synagogues took on the appearance of barns so as not be conspicuous. To avoid competition with the churches located in the centre of town, synagogues were usually erected in areas reserved for the Jewish quarter. But there are conflicting stories about where Jews lived. According to some people we interviewed, Jews were scattered throughout the village and lived wherever their shops were located. Others claimed Jews lived in specific areas. In either case, for safety, buildings were enclosed and monumental. There were often no significant details on the facade to identify them.[8]

Joyce Ellen Weinstein.

[66] Wooden synagogue, Zeizmariai, 2002.
This is the perfect shtetl one dreams of. No Soviet blocks, pure shtetl.

1. Israel in Lithuania
2. Agudat Yisrael

[67]
Inside the Zeizmariai Synagogue, 2002.
There were small fragments of posters in Hebrew writing on the walls so it felt recent and eerie. It would have been Yiddish.

Kurkliai

[68] Wooden synagogue in field, Kurkliai, 2003.
Some interesting old houses nearby in village. Such a lovely shtetl. A little brook runs near the synagogue. Such a lovely day with butterflies everywhere. It looks so sad.

Zeizmariai

[69] Wooden houses, typical shtetl, Zeizmariai, 2002.
Jewish houses usually had steps to the door, no porches. This one is a late addition.

Plunge

[70]
Mass graves, Plunge, 2004.
Plunge's Jewish population of 1,700 Jews was murdered here by the Nazis – on 15 and 16 July, 1941.

Palanga

[71]
Forest, Palanga, 2003.
I was cycling through the forest when, all of a sudden, I came across Jewish gravestones. I began to examine them when a snake hissed at me and I fled.

Ponary

[72]
Killing fields of Ponary, 2004.
Ponary, a small desolate village some ten kilometres from Vilna, was the most notorious of killing sites. It was not itself a community but will always be sacred in memory of the Jews of Vilna. Some 70,000-100,000 people were murdered here by the Nazis, with the help of Lithuanian collaborators. Most of those who died were Jews. The majority were shot and buried in large pits that the Soviets had built for storage tanks.

In September 1943 the Nazis began burning the evidence of their mass murder. It was in the forest named after the village where many Jews were killed. In his call to resistance the Vilna poet, Abba Kovner, wrote:

Whoever is taken through the gate of the ghetto has only one road ahead – Ponary. And Ponary is death. Better to fall with honour in the Ghetto than be led like sheep to Ponary.

Plateliai

[73] Wooden house in Plateliai's main square, 2003.
Positioned on the crossroads leading to Salantai. Two windows are next to each other, allowing the residents to call it one window, so they would pay less tax.

[74] Jewish house with alterations, Plateliai, 2003.
House in Plateliai's main street. The porch was added later. Opposite the house a volunteer in the World Christian Mission, was canvassing for road humps to be put in to prevent wild motorbikers from riding up and down. Many drunks around. Tourist area, beautiful lakes.

Dorbian

[75]
House next to cemetery,
Dorbian, 2002.

[76]
Non-Jewish home in
Dorbian, 2002.
Note the porch.

[77]
Woman sitting outside house next to Dorbian cemetery, 2003.

[78]
'New' Dorbian cemetery, 2004.
New from 1895. We spent hours here looking for our family, the Seligs of Dorbian. We found one stone with Selig on the tombstone. The mayor of Dorbian took us to the older cemetery near Laukzeme by horse and cart. Laukzeme was where the Jews lived in the 1600s before they moved to Dorbian.

[79] Matzo maker of Dorbian, 2004.
He baked matzo for Jews and worked for one of my relatives "Jewish Selig" who had a shop which sold scarves. Then he asked my brother, whether he was a Lithuanian or a Zhyd (Jew). He had once had a Jewish girlfriend – Malka Pucca. The Jewish girls taught him Jewish songs. He wanted to marry Malka, but his father would not let him. Then the Germans came and killed the Jews and they cried very much. If it had not been for the war he would have married her, he said. He remembers the Germans torturing the Jews, putting cigarettes in their mouths and shooting them. Some 300 Jews were taken to be shot, he said.

[80] Two old Dorbian residents, 2004.
He kicked her when she said they bought the house from Jews in 1946. It was my grandmother's shtetl. I wondered if my grandmother had lived there. The woman said she had been sent to Dorbian by the Russians from Memel after the war and they had given her the house. I saw her next in an urn.

[81] Woman in her home, 2004.

[82] Dorbian, green doors, 2004.

[83] Backyard where Sukkah would have stood, Dorbian, 2004.
They said: "strange people once lived there. They sat for a week in an open room each year. We had to put the roof on top." This would have been a sukkah.

[84] Street where my grandmother lived, Dorbian, 2004.
My grandmother must have walked here. Was this Freda Zeligas's house or Selig as they became?

Vaitimenai

[85]
Looking through the window into a house in Vaitimenai,
Greville Janner's shtetl, 2004.

[86]
Alderman's house, Vaitimenai, 2004.
Alderman's house. Had it been a church or a synagogue? Only about four houses there. Greville held his hand up to the sky and said: "Grandpa, I've come home. Can you hear me? Are you proud of me?" And then he plucked apples from a tree and took one for each grandchild.

[87]
Old house, Vaitimenai, 2004.

[88] Door of house, in Vaitimenai, 2004.

Laukuva

[89]
Laukuva Synagogue, 2004.
I could immediately make out the women's entrance to the synagogue in this empty little village. Notice the steps up from the side.

Resainai

[90]
House, Resainiai, 2004.

Luoke

[91] Typical shop in Luoke, 2004.
I liked it. Typical. Beautiful green door. They cut off the corner. Jewish shops were often located on street corners to make them visible from two streets. It was good for business. Perhaps it meant they could escape down either street if there was trouble.

[92] Green door of corner shop in Luoke, 2004.

Rietavas

[93] Market square, with church, Rietavas, 2004.

[94] Forest – near Skuodas, 2004.
We were near the killing field in Skuodas. I was drawn to it because many of my ancestors came from here including two of the town's spiritual leaders, Reb Aharon Horowitz and Reb Yisroel Zelig.

[95] Bathers at Palanga beach, 2004. Everyone comes here for the sandy beaches. My grandmother would visit from Dorbian. Amber is everywhere. The beach is lined by trees. The Amber Museum here was run by Jews.

Kaunas
(Kovno)

There have been Jews in Kaunas since the 15th century, although at times they were persecuted by the city authorities and forced to find refuge in the neighbouring community of Slobodka. Although theoretically a distinct community, in many ways Slobodka acted as a suburb of Kaunas. Relations between the Jewish and non-Jewish inhabitants of the city continued to be bad throughout the 18th century, and it was not until the early 19th century that the Jews could be considered as having finally established themselves there.

Economic conditions improved to some extent for the Jews during the second half of the nineteenth century; the main road and railway lines to St Petersburg provided work for many in the city as did the construction of an elaborate system of fortifications around the city. But many Jews still lived in conditions of abject poverty, and emigration was an important feature of Jewish life. There were a number of religious schools and other institutions, and one of the rabbis in the community, Rabbi Yitzhak-Elhanan Spector, had influence all over Europe. When, for example, there was a conflict in London over the standards of shechitah (religious slaughter) as performed locally, the protagonist on each side appealed to Rabbi Spector for his official adjudication.

After the seizure of Vilna by the Poles, Kaunas became the capital of Lithuania, and by 1940 there were about 40,000 Jews in the city out of a total population of about 160,000. The city had almost 100 Jewish organisations, forty synagogues, many Yiddish schools, four Hebrew high schools, a Jewish hospital, and scores of Jewish-owned businesses. It was also an important Zionist centre. When Russia took over, much of the Jewish structure of the city was closed down, and a week before the German invasion hundreds of Jewish families were arrested and exiled to Siberia. The Germans entered Kaunas on 24th June 1941, but even before their arrival bands of Lithuanians began to murder Jews in Kaunas and Slobodka. The Germans moved many Jews to one or other of the Forts around the city, mainly the infamous Fort Nine where many thousands were slaughtered. (See Ninth Fort drawing for more information.) The Kovno ghetto was established and then a concentration camp. After the war there were some 2,000 surviving Kaunas Jews. Now the Jewish population has dwindled to around 500. One synagogue remains in use.

[96] Shtetl, Jurbarkas Street, Slobodka, Kaunas, 2004.
Miserable day. It matches the feeling I have about the place. I can't wait to get out. Pogrom on 26 June '41. 1,000 people killed. The head of Rabbi Oforski was exhibited on the second floor – shown here with a little arrow on the right.

[97]
Kaunas Synagogue with aeroplane, 2004.

[98]
Vytauto 58, house of Moriah Rabinowitz, Kaunas, 2004.
Owned by family owners of knitting wire plant – perished in the Ninth Fort. Magnificent, art nouveau/Bauhaus influences.

[99]
Kaunas Synagogue
– interior, 2004.

[100]
Main Jewish hospital, Kaunas, 2004.
On this cold damp day I can see all the poor Jewish people traipsing into this bedraggled, once fine-looking building – today it is for sale for 300,000 euros.

[101]
Zamenhof Street,
Synagogue,
Kaunas, 2004.
I guessed it was a shul –
and it was! Zamenhof was
the inventor of Esperanto.
He sought to unite people
divided by ethnicity and
language. All over Poland
and Lithuania there are
streets named after him.
He also wrote a Yiddish
grammar book – which is
still unpublished.

[102]
Hassidic Synagogue,
Kaunas, 2004.
Now a pub? I had no
time to sketch this
slowly. It was raining.

[103]
Spector's Orphanage, Kaunas, 2004.
Yitzhak-Elhanan Spector's orphanage. Founded after his death in 1900. Various institutions were named after him. He was one of the most prominent rabbis of Lithuanian Jewry in the 19th century. Chief Rabbi of Kovno. Lived 1817-1896.

[104]
Professor Leah Goldberg's house, Kaunas, 2004.
Born in Kovno in 1911 poet and writer Leah Goldberg studied at Lithuanian and German universities before leaving for Israel in 1935. Her poems are known for their melancholy subjects with positive messages.

[105] Synagogue next to house of Minkowski brothers, 2004. Oskar and Hermann Minkowski were both noted scholars. Hermann was a theoretical mathematician who taught Einstein mathematics and helped develop Einstein's theory of general relativity. Oskar introduced the concept that diabetes results from suppression of pancreatic substances – later found to be the hormone insulin.

[106] Rabbi Grodzinski's house, Kaunas, 2004.
Avram Grodzinski helped build Hebron in Palestine 1925. He was burnt by the Nazis in the Kovno ghetto. Notice that the windows are next to each other which means they paid less tax.

The Ninth Fort, Kaunas.

"It was a short shuffle from the front gate down the Path of Death to the Wall of Death, a corner of a moat like trench where people were lined up as targets and shot. Today this wall is still riddled with bullet holes and is the fort's starkest reminder of the evil that was perpetarted here In all, some 80,000 people from Lithuania, Austria, France, and other Nazi occupied areas, were slaughtered at the Ninth fort, including most of Kovno's population. Just behind the trench is a field where the dead were discarded. Today, it is a peaceful spread of green back-dropped by a new housing development. Adjacent to the field is the leviathan Monument to the Victims of Fascism, a concrete crush of desperate faces rising from the earth in immortal resistance. Behind the synagogue stands a memorial to the 1,800 children who were murdered here."[9]

Jono David

[107] The Ninth Fort, Kaunas, 2004.
I didn't want to draw this but Aubrey insisted. No words are needed.

[108] Forest near where I was lost, Ukmerge, 2002.

[109] Door in Jewish Museum, Vilnius, 2002.

[110] Staircase, Museum, 2002.

[111]
Doors to home next to synago[gue]
Zeizmariai, 2004.

[112] Interior of home next to synagogue, Zeizmariai, 2004.

[113]
Woman of Telz and red door, 2002.
I was with a group when we passed by the house with yellow doors. It had been a Jewish home once. They all said: "You can't do that!" as I knocked on her door. I took photographs. I had no time to sketch. I then followed the group down the street to the lake, along the same route where the Jews were marched down and shot by Nazis and Lithuanian collaborators.

[114]
Doors leading to resident
of Darbenai, 2004.

You can see in this painting that one of the women had deformities to her left arm. It was typical of terrible deformities among the elderly.

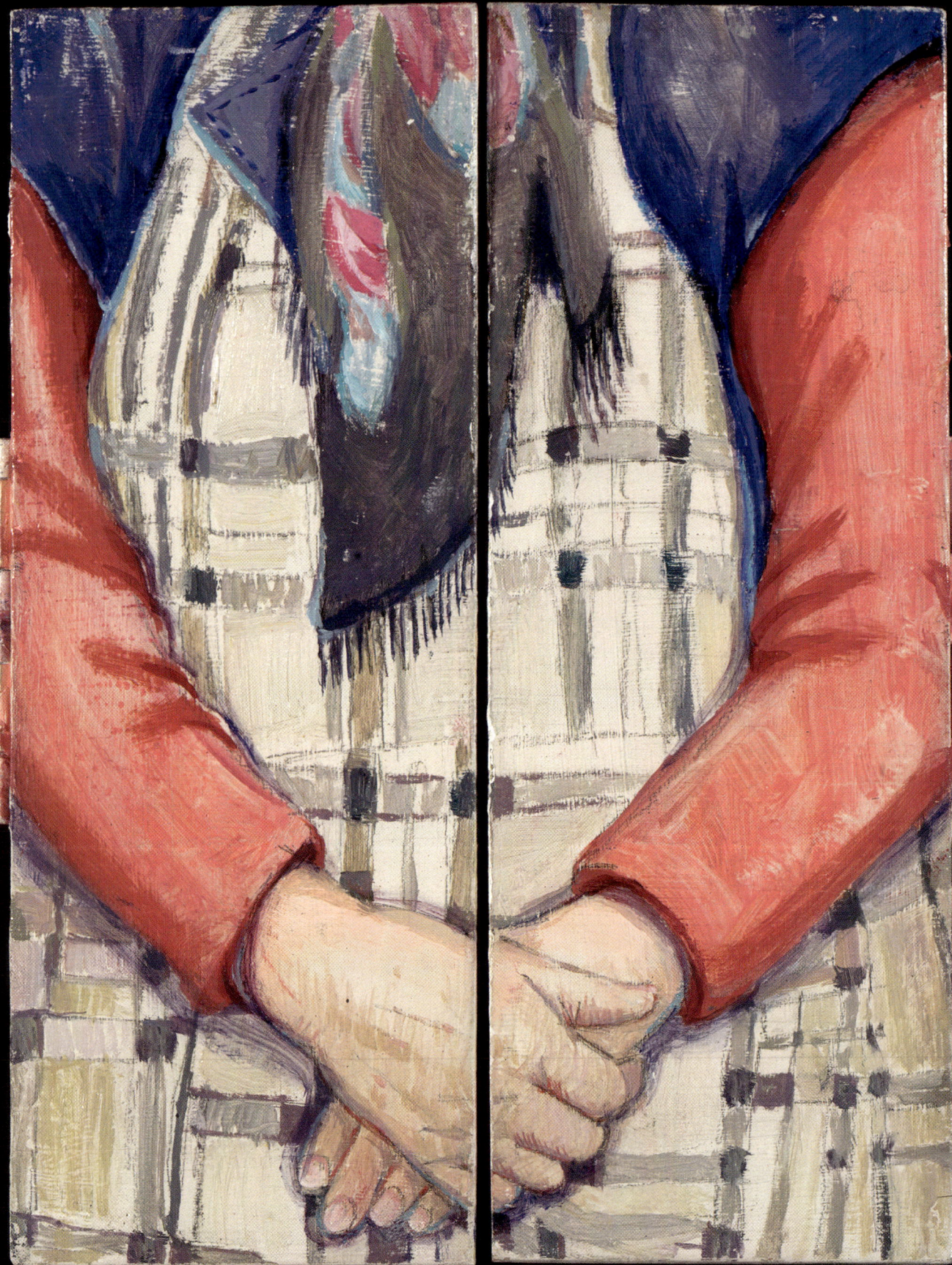

[117] Woman with open hands (blessing the Sabbath candles), 2004.

[118]
Woman whose parents hid Jewish family, Plokstine, 2004.
We went to a nearby farmer in Plokstine who had a ramshackle hut where he did woodwork. He had Jewish artefacts. He said he had found them in a broken-down Jewish home in Plunge. I bought a paper knife from him, made in Memel in 1928.

[119]
Woman with milk pail, Liubavas, 2004.

[120]
Man in red braces, keeper of Jewish cemetery, Darbenai, 2004.

[121] Woman of Telz, 2004.

[122] Woman in front of her oven, Zeizmariai, 2004.

[123] Woman in Skuados with red-squared carpet, 2004.

[124] Boy in doorway with green door, Darbenai, 2004.

[125] Girl in Bedroom, Darbenai, 2004.
The child in the drawing was actually a boy, not a girl. When I came back the following year he was dead. Some old people pointed to the ground when I asked where he was.

[127]
Possibly my ancestral home in Darbenai with my daughter and her children, 2004.

[128] Open doors to staircase of the Jewish museum, Vilnius, 2004.

[132] Woman in in Jewish dentist's house, Slobodka, 2003.

[133] My grandmother, Freda Selig from Dorbian, at her new home in Newcastle England, 2004.
She came from Dorbian in 1898. She left when she was eighteen. The rest of the family who left, came bit by bit. She saved sixpence a week to help bring them over. Like many Jews from north west Lithuania she emigrated to the north east of England. Most of the others settled in South Africa. The exodus began when Kretinga market square burnt down in 1899. Many local shtetls lost their businesses to other markets.

[134] Forest near Nemencine, with lake, 2005.

[135] Vilna Gaon's grave - showing graves on side of canvas, 2003.

[136] Vilna Gaon's grave, 2003.

[137] Rosengarten family's last Passover meal, c. 1985.
This is actually based on a photograph of my husband's family, the Rosengartens at their last Passover supper before the war, deciding whether to leave for England. I include it here because it demonstrates the tragic end for the Jews of the Baltic lands.

[138] Discussions on emigrating, 1981.
Tea party where the Rosengarten family discuss who is going to leave and who is going to stay.

[139] Birch Trees, Palanga, 2003.

Catalogue of works

Dimensions are given in inches – height before width

1
Vilna Gaon's Grave in Vilnius Cemetery
2002
pencil on paper
7 x 7

2
Old street, Vilnius – with arch
2002
pencil on paper
6 x 4

3
Oldest synagogue in Vilnius, 6 Guilu Street
2002
Pencil on paper
6 x 4.5

4
Oldest synagogue in Vilnius – side view
2002
Pencil on paper
4.5 x 6

5
Locked in Choral Synagogue, Vilnius
2002
Pencil on paper
7 x 7

6
Choral synagogue Vilnius – entrance
2002
Pencil on paper
6 x 4

7
Inside corridor of Choral Synagogue
2003
Ink on paper
6 x 4.5

8
Ghetto of Vilnius, House, 10 Rudnuha
2003
Pencil on paper
7 x 7

9
Synagogue – back entrance, Pilymo Street, Vilnius
2002
Pencil on paper
4 x 6

10
Jewish homes behind synagogue in Pilymo Street, Vilnius
2002
Pencil on paper
6 x 4

11
Jewish home behind synagogue in Pilymo Street, Vilnius
2002
Pencil on paper
4 x 6

12
Woman carrying sack, Vilnius
2002
Pencil on paper
6 x 4

13
St Casimir's Church. Built 1604, Vilnius
2002
Pencil on paper
4 x 6

14
Jewish Museum bannisters – was Hebrew School, Vilnius
2002
Pencil on paper
6 x 4

15
Back of Hebrew School/Jewish Museum. View from office, Vilnius
2004
Pencil on paper
5 x 5

16
Looking out of Jewish Museum, Vilnius
2002
Pencil on paper
4 x 6

17
Homes next to Vilna Gaon's house, with statue, Vilnius
2002
Pencil on paper
7 x 7

18
Zemaitijos Street, Vilnius
2003
Ink on paper
4.5 x 6

19
Mother and two children, Zeizmariai
2004
Watercolour
6 x 4

20
Woman cleaning window, Uzipos, Vilnius
2004
Pencil on paper
5 x 5

21
House and synagogue in Uzipos, with alterations, Vilnius
2004
Pencil on Paper
5 x 5

22
Synagogue in Uzipos, Vilnius
2004
Pencil on Paper
7 x 7

23
Courtyard of Choral Synagogue, Vilnius
2003
Pencil on paper
7 x 7

24
100th Anniversary celebrations in Choral Synagogue, Vilnius
2003
pencil on paper
4.5 x 6

25
Choral Synagogue, Vilnius
2004
Watercolour
5.5 x 7

26
Europas Parkas – stone sculpture (1)
2002
Pencil on paper
4 x 4

27
Europas Parkas – stone sculpture (2)
2002
Pencil on paper
4 x 4

28
Europas Parkas – outside the restaurant
2002
Pencil on paper
4.5 x 6

29
Lake and swimmers at the Green Lakes near Europas Parkas
2002
Pencil on paper.
4 x 6

30
Europas Parkas – house where I lived
2002
Pencil on paper
4 x 4

31
Farmstead. Man with scythe near Europas Parkas, Skirgiskes
2002
Pencil on paper
4 x 4

32
The mill house near Europas Parkas
2003
Watercolour
4.5 x 6

33
House in Liubavas. Owner was sent to Siberia, near Europas Parkas
2003
Pencil on paper
7 x 7

34
Woman resting after potato pickings near Europas Parkas
2003
Watercolour
4.5 x 6

35
Woman doing washing, Liubavas
2002
Pencil on paper
6 x 4.5

36
Disabled woman outside house next to pond, Liubavas
2002
Ink on paper
4 x 6

37
Europas Parkas – lost in woods
2003
Ink on paper
4.5 x 6

38
House in Liubavas
2002
Pencil on paper
4 x 6

39
Old chapel, Liubavas
2002
Pencil on Paper
4 x 6

40
Home of elderly lady, Liubavas
2002
Pencil on Paper
4 x 6

41
Little girl and house, Liubavas
2002
Pencil on paper
4 x 6

42
A soldier folds his arm at the fair at Kernave
2002
4 x 6
Pencil on paper

43
Fair at Kernave
2002
Ink on paper
4 x 6

44
A non-Jewish home, Kernave
2002
Pencil on paper
4 x 6

45
Chickens next to old church near Trakai
2002
Pencil on paper
4 x 4

46
Church near Trakai
2002
Pencil on paper
4 x 4

47
Karaite house of prayer Trakai
2002
Ink on paper
7 x 7

48
Exterior of Karaite prayer house, Trakai
2002
Ink on paper
7 x 7

49
Old house in Nemencine
2003
Pencil on paper
4.5 x 6

50
Church in Nemencine, near Europas Parkas
2003
Pencil on paper
6 x 4.5

51
Two women with pails, Nemencine
2003
Watercolour
4 x 6

52
Woman with horse and cow
2004
Watercolour
4 x 6

53
Building, Glitiskes near Paberze
2002
Pencil on paper
7 x 7

54
Ukmerge Synagogue
2003
Pencil on paper
7 x 7

55
Reitavas Synagogue
2004
Pencil on paper
4 x 6

56
Doors of collapsing old house, Jew Street, Kedainiai
2004
Pencil on paper
4 x 6

57
Mustard house in Zydu Street, Kedainiai
2004
Watercolour
4 x 6

58
Two synagogues, Kedainiai
2004
Pencil on paper
5 x 5

59
"Jewish" oven, Dorbian
2004
Watercolour
4 x 6

60
Oven, Zeizmariai
2002
Pencil on paper
7 x 7

61
Woman by oven in house in Jewish district, Slobodka, Kaunas
2004
Pencil on paper
7 x 7

62
Oven, Dorbian
2002
Pencil on paper
7 x 7

63
Woman in room, Slobodka, Kaunas
2004
Pencil on paper
7 x 7

64
Woman in kitchen, Slobodka, Kaunas
2004
Pencil on paper
7 x 7

65
Pokroijos Synagogue
2003
Pencil on paper
4.5 x 6

66
Wooden synagogue, Zeizmariai
2002
Pencil on paper
7 x 7

67
Inside the Zeizmariai Synagogue (includes Pic of fragment)
2002
Pencil on paper
7 x 7

68
Wooden synagogue in field, Kurkliai
2003
Pencil on paper
7 x 7

69
Wooden houses, typical shtetl. Zeizmariai
2002
Pencil on paper
7 x 7

70
Mass graves, Plunge
2004
Pen on paper
4 x 6

71
Forest, Palanga
2003
Pencil on paper
4.5 x 6

72
Killing fields of Ponary
2004
Watercolour
6 x 4

73
Wooden house in Plateliai's main square
2003
Pencil on paper
7 x 7

74
Jewish house with alterations, Plateliai
2003
Pencil on paper
7 x 7

75
House next to cemetery, Dorbian
2002
Pencil on paper
7 x 7

76
Non-Jewish home in Dorbian
2002
Pencil on paper
7 x 7

77
Woman sitting outside house next to Dorbian cemetery
2003
Pencil on paper
5 x 5

78
"New" Dorbian cemetery
2004
Pencil on paper
4 x 6

79
Matzo maker of Dorbian
2004
Watercolour
6 x 4

80
Two old Dorbian residents
2004
Watercolour
4 x 6

81
Woman in her home
2004
Watercolour
6 x 4

82
Dorbian, green doors
2004
Watercolour
4 x 6

83
Backyard where Sukkah would have stood, Dorbian
2004.
Watercolour
4 x 6

84
Street where my grandmother lived, Dorbian
2004
Watercolour
4 x 6

85
Looking through the window into a house in Vaitimenai, Greville Janner's shtetl
2004
Watercolour
4 x 6

86
Alderman's house, Vaitimenai
2004
Pencil on paper
4 x 6

87
Old house, Vaitimenai
2004
Pencil on paper
4 x 6

88
Door of house in Vaitimenai
2004
Watercolour
6 x 4

89
Laukuva Synagogue
2004
Pencil on paper
4 x 6

90
House, Resainiai
2004
Pencil on paper
4 x 6

91
Typical shop in Luoke
2004
Pencil on paper
4 x 6

92
Green door of corner shop in Luoke
2004
Watercolour
6 x 4

93
Market square, with church, Rietavas
2004
Pencil on paper
4 x 6

94
Forest – near Skuodas
2004
Pen on paper
4 x 6

95
Bathers at Palanga beach
2004
Pencil on paper
4 x 6

96
Shtetl, Jurbarkas Street, Slobodka, Kaunas
2004
Pencil on paper
7 x 7

97
Kaunas Synagogue with aeroplane
2004
Pencil on paper
7 x 7

98
Vytauto 58, house of Moriah Rabinowitz, Kaunas
2004
Pencil on paper
5 x 5

99
Kaunas Synagogue – interior
2004
Pen on paper
7 x 7

100
Main Jewish hospital, Kaunas
2004
Pencil on paper
7 x 7

101
Zhaminof Street, Synagogue, Kaunas
2004
Pencil on paper
5 x 5

102
Hassidic Synagogue, Kaunas
2004
Pencil on paper
5 x 5

103
Spector's Orphanage, Kaunas
2004
Pencil on paper
5 x 5

104
Professor Leah Goldberg's house, Kaunas
2004
Pencil on paper
5 x 5

105
Synagogue next to house of Minkovski brothers
2004
Pencil on paper
5 x 5

106
Rabbi Grodzinski's house, Kaunas
2004
Pencil on paper
5 x 5

107
The Ninth Fort, Kaunas
2004
Pencil on paper
5 x 5

108
Forest near where I was lost, Ukmerge
2002
Oil on wood
4 x 20

109
Doors in Jewish Museum, Vilnius
2002
Oil on wood – triptych
10 x 8 (closed)

110
Staircase of Jewish Museum, Vilnius
2002
Oil on wood – triptych
10 x 8 (gatefold opens to 20 inches wide)

111
Doors to home next to synagogue, Zeizmariai
2004
Oil on wood – triptych
8 x 10 (closed)

112
Interior of home next to synagogue, Zeizmariai
2004
Oil on wood – triptych
8 x 20 (opened)
Collection of Mr and Mrs Townley

113
Woman of Telz and red door
2002
Oil on wood – triptych
8 x 12 (opened)

114
Doors leading to residents of Darbenai
2004
Oil on wood – triptych
8 x 10 (closed)

115
Residents of Darbenai
2004
Oil on wood – triptych
8 x 20 (opened)

116
Woman about to bring in the Sabbath
2004
Oil on wood – triptych
6 x 8 (closed)

117
Woman with open hands (blessing the Sabbath candles)
2004
Oil on wood – triptych
6 x 12 (opened)

118
Woman whose parents hid Jewish family, Plokstine
2004
Pastel on paper
28.5 x 13

119
Woman with milk pail, Liubavas
2004
Pastel on paper
28 x 6.5

120
Man in red braces, keeper of Jewish cemetery, Darbenai
2004
Pastel on paper
28 x 6.5

121
Woman of Telz
2004
Pastel on paper
33 x 24

122
Woman in front of her oven, Zeizmariai
2004
Pastel on paper
27 x 19
Collection Jeanette Copperman

123
Woman in Skuados with red-squared carpet
2004
Pastel on paper
29.5 x 22

124
Boy in doorway with green door, Darbenai
2004
Pastel on paper
29.5 x 23

125
Girl in Bedroom, Darbenai
2004
Pastel on paper
33 x 24

126
Doors to Triptych
2004
Oil on wood – triptych
8 x 6 (closed)

127
Possibly my ancestral home in Darbenai with my daughter and her children
2004
Pastel on paper
27.5 x 40

128
Open doors to staircase of the Jewish museum, Vilnius.
2004
Oil on wood – triptych

129
Staircase to Jewish Museum, Vilnius.
2003
Oil on canvas
12 x 8

130
Kitchen interior, Zeimariai
2003
Oil on wood
8 x 10

131
Synagogue, Guilu Street, Vilnius
2004
Oil on canvas
10 x 12

132
Woman in Jewish dentist's house, Slobodka
2003
Oil on canvas
24 x 20

133
My grandmother, Freda Selig from Dorbian
1985
Oil on board
Collection Marian Stern
28 x 28

134
Forest near Nemencine, with lake
2005
Oil on wood – triptych
10 x 24 (opened)

135
Vilna Gaon's grave - showing graves on side of canvas
2003
Oil on canvas
5 x 4

136
Vilna Gaon's grave
2003
Oil on canvas
5 x 4

137
Rosengarten family's last Passover meal
c. 1985
Oil on canvas
24 x 36
Collection Eugene Dattel. New York

138
Discussions on emigrating
1981
Oil on board
48 x 36

139
Birch Trees, Palanga
2003
oil on wood
3 x 15
Collection Mr and Mrs Anton Curtis.

[138] Discussions on emigrating, 1981.
Tea party where the Rosengarten family discuss who is going to leave and who is going to stay.

References

1. This timeline by Aubrey Newman first appeared in Jewish Rennaissance, July 2005.

2. From information supplied by: Professor Aubrey Newman; The City Paper, The Baltic States, article on "Jewish Vilnius"; and Edward Serrota, Centropa Quarterly, Winter 2005.

3. Jews in Lithuania website, © Jews in Lithuania, Vilnius, 1999-2000.

4. Marija Rupeikiene and others, Lithuanian Synagogues Exhibitions Guide, 1997.

5. From Betty Birsky's article Two Lithuanian Stories, Journal of the South Pacific Association for Commonwealth Literature and Language Studies, Number 36 (1993).

6. Chaim Yaakov Epstein wrote this seventy years ago. Translated in 1990 by Meyer Dwass.

7. From the Autobiography of Jacob Hyam Rubenstein, 1890-1963. Source: ShtetLinks, Vishtinetz, Lithuania.

8. Joyce Ellen Weinstein. Article on wooden synagogues, Zeek magazine, October 2005.

9. From "The Jews of Kovno" by Jono David in the Jewish Magazine. Aug-Sept 2000. Issue 35.

Credits

We would like to thank Jewish Renniassance magazine for allowing us to use the timeline by Aubrey Newman; The City Paper, The Baltic States for the information on Vilnius; the Virtual Jewish Library and the American Israeli Co-operative Enterprise for Jono David's article on the Jews of Kovno; the Association of Lithuanian Jews in Israel for information relating to Raseiniai that appeared in Lithuanian Jewry Vol. 3, and for the translation by Jonathan Levitow. Our thanks also to Betty Birsky and the JSPA for her contribution, and also to Joyce Ellen Weinstein and Zeek magazine, Meyer Dwass and Marija Rupeikiene.